MW00936374

This
Poetry Notebook
belongs to:

_____

FIND INSPIRATION

WEATHER

_____
_____
_____

SEASON

_____
_____
_____

SIGHTS

_____
_____
_____

SMELL

_____
_____
_____

SOUNDS

_____
_____
_____

TASTE

_____
_____
_____

TOUCH

_____
_____
_____

PEOPLE

_____
_____
_____

BOOKS

_____
_____
_____

EVENTS

_____
_____
_____

DREAMS

_____
_____

IMAGINATION

_____
_____

DRAFT INSPIRATION

FIGURATIVE LANGUAGE:

1. SIMILE (USE LIKE OR AS)

2. METAPHOR (SAYING ONE IS ANOTHER)

3. PERSONIFICATION(HUMANIZE STUFF)

WRITE NOW & WRITE FREELY

FIND INSPIRATION

WEATHER

_____

_____

_____

SEASON

_____

_____

_____

SIGHTS

_____

_____

_____

SMELL

_____

_____

_____

SOUNDS

_____

_____

_____

TASTE

_____

_____

_____

TOUCH

_____

_____

_____

PEOPLE

_____

_____

_____

BOOKS

_____

_____

_____

EVENTS

_____

_____

_____

DREAMS

_____

_____

IMAGINATION

_____

_____

DRAFT INSPIRATION

FIGURATIVE LANGUAGE:

1.SIMILE (USE LIKE OR AS)

2.METAPHOR (SAYING ONE IS ANOTHER)

3.PERSONIFICATION(HUMANIZE STUFF)

WRITE NOW & WRITE FREELY

FIND INSPIRATION

WEATHER

_____

_____

_____

SIGHTS

_____

_____

_____

SOUNDS

_____

_____

_____

TOUCH

_____

_____

_____

BOOKS

_____

_____

_____

DREAMS

_____

_____

SEASON

_____

_____

_____

SMELL

_____

_____

_____

TASTE

_____

_____

_____

PEOPLE

_____

_____

_____

EVENTS

_____

_____

_____

IMAGINATION

_____

_____

DRAFT INSPIRATION

FIGURATIVE LANGUAGE:

.SIMILE (USE LIKE OR AS)

.METAPHOR (SAYING ONE IS ANOTHER)

.PERSONIFICATION(HUMANIZE STUFF)

WRITE NOW & WRITE FREELY

FIND INSPIRATION

WEATHER	SEASON
SIGHTS	SMELL
SOUNDS	TASTE
TOUCH	PEOPLE
BOOKS	EVENTS
DREAMS	IMAGINATION

DRAFT INSPIRATION

FIGURATIVE LANGUAGE:

1. SIMILE (USE LIKE OR AS)

2. METAPHOR (SAYING ONE IS ANOTHER)

3. PERSONIFICATION(HUMANIZE STUFF)

WRITE NOW & WRITE FREELY

FIND INSPIRATION

WEATHER

SEASON

SIGHTS

SMELL

SOUNDS

TASTE

TOUCH

PEOPLE

BOOKS

EVENTS

DREAMS

IMAGINATION

DRAFT INSPIRATION

FIGURATIVE LANGUAGE:

1.SIMILE (USE LIKE OR AS)

2.METAPHOR (SAYING ONE IS ANOTHER)

3.PERSONIFICATION(HUMANIZE STUFF)

WRITE NOW & WRITE FREELY

FIND INSPIRATION

WEATHER

SEASON

SIGHTS

SMELL

SOUNDS

TASTE

TOUCH

PEOPLE

BOOKS

EVENTS

DREAMS

IMAGINATION

DRAFT INSPIRATION

FIGURATIVE LANGUAGE:

.SIMILE (USE LIKE OR AS)

.METAPHOR (SAYING ONE IS ANOTHER)

.PERSONIFICATION(HUMANIZE STUFF)

WRITE NOW & WRITE FREELY

FIND INSPIRATION

WEATHER

SEASON

SIGHTS

SMELL

SOUNDS

TASTE

TOUCH

PEOPLE

BOOKS

EVENTS

DREAMS

IMAGINATION

DRAFT INSPIRATION

FIGURATIVE LANGUAGE:

1.SIMILE (USE LIKE OR AS)

2.METAPHOR (SAYING ONE IS ANOTHER)

3.PERSONIFICATION(HUMANIZE STUFF)

WRITE NOW & WRITE FREELY

FIND INSPIRATION

WEATHER

SEASON

SIGHTS

SMELL

SOUNDS

TASTE

TOUCH

PEOPLE

BOOKS

EVENTS

DREAMS

IMAGINATION

DRAFT INSPIRATION

FIGURATIVE LANGUAGE:

1.SIMILE (USE LIKE OR AS)

_____

_____

_____

2.METAPHOR (SAYING ONE IS ANOTHER)

_____

_____

3.PERSONIFICATION(HUMANIZE STUFF)

_____

_____

_____

WRITE NOW & WRITE FREELY

_____

_____

_____

_____

_____

_____

_____

_____

_____

_____

_____

_____

_____

_____

FIND INSPIRATION

WEATHER

_____

SEASON

_____

SIGHTS

_____

SMELL

_____

SOUNDS

_____

TASTE

_____

TOUCH

_____

PEOPLE

_____

BOOKS

_____

EVENTS

_____

DREAMS

_____

IMAGINATION

_____

DRAFT INSPIRATION
IGURATIVE LANGUAGE:
.SIMILE (USE LIKE OR AS)

.METAPHOR (SAYING ONE IS ANOTHER)

.PERSONIFICATION(HUMANIZE STUFF)

/RITE NOW & WRITE FREELY

FIND INSPIRATION

WEATHER	SEASON
SIGHTS	SMELL
SOUNDS	TASTE
TOUCH	PEOPLE
BOOKS	EVENTS
DREAMS	IMAGINATION

DRAFT INSPIRATION

FIGURATIVE LANGUAGE:

1.SIMILE (USE LIKE OR AS)

2.METAPHOR (SAYING ONE IS ANOTHER)

3.PERSONIFICATION(HUMANIZE STUFF)

WRITE NOW & WRITE FREELY

FIND INSPIRATION

WEATHER

_____

_____

_____

SEASON

_____

_____

_____

SIGHTS

_____

_____

_____

SMELL

_____

_____

_____

SOUNDS

_____

_____

_____

TASTE

_____

_____

_____

TOUCH

_____

_____

_____

PEOPLE

_____

_____

_____

BOOKS

_____

_____

_____

EVENTS

_____

_____

_____

DREAMS

_____

_____

IMAGINATION

_____

_____

DRAFT INSPIRATION

FIGURATIVE LANGUAGE:

.SIMILE (USE LIKE OR AS)

.METAPHOR (SAYING ONE IS ANOTHER)

.PERSONIFICATION(HUMANIZE STUFF)

WRITE NOW & WRITE FREELY

FIND INSPIRATION

WEATHER

SEASON

SIGHTS

SMELL

SOUNDS

TASTE

TOUCH

PEOPLE

BOOKS

EVENTS

DREAMS

IMAGINATION

DRAFT INSPIRATION

IGURATIVE LANGUAGE:

.SIMILE (USE LIKE OR AS)

.METAPHOR (SAYING ONE IS ANOTHER)

.PERSONIFICATION(HUMANIZE STUFF)

/RITE NOW & WRITE FREELY

FIND INSPIRATION

WEATHER

SEASON

SIGHTS

SMELL

SOUNDS

TASTE

TOUCH

PEOPLE

BOOKS

EVENTS

DREAMS

IMAGINATION

DRAFT INSPIRATION

FIGURATIVE LANGUAGE:

1.SIMILE (USE LIKE OR AS)

2.METAPHOR (SAYING ONE IS ANOTHER)

3.PERSONIFICATION(HUMANIZE STUFF)

WRITE NOW & WRITE FREELY

FIND INSPIRATION

WEATHER

SEASON

SIGHTS

SMELL

SOUNDS

TASTE

TOUCH

PEOPLE

BOOKS

EVENTS

DREAMS

IMAGINATION

DRAFT INSPIRATION

FIGURATIVE LANGUAGE:

.SIMILE (USE LIKE OR AS)

_____

_____

.METAPHOR (SAYING ONE IS ANOTHER)

_____

_____

.PERSONIFICATION(HUMANIZE STUFF)

_____

_____

WRITE NOW & WRITE FREELY

_____

_____

_____

_____

_____

_____

_____

_____

_____

_____

_____

_____

_____

FIND INSPIRATION

WEATHER

_____

_____

_____

SEASON

_____

_____

_____

SIGHTS

_____

_____

_____

SMELL

_____

_____

_____

SOUNDS

_____

_____

_____

TASTE

_____

_____

_____

TOUCH

_____

_____

_____

PEOPLE

_____

_____

_____

BOOKS

_____

_____

_____

EVENTS

_____

_____

_____

DREAMS

_____

_____

IMAGINATION

_____

_____

DRAFT INSPIRATION

IGURATIVE LANGUAGE:

.SIMILE (USE LIKE OR AS)

.METAPHOR (SAYING ONE IS ANOTHER)

.PERSONIFICATION(HUMANIZE STUFF)

/RITE NOW & WRITE FREELY

FIND INSPIRATION

WEATHER

SEASON

SIGHTS

SMELL

SOUNDS

TASTE

TOUCH

PEOPLE

BOOKS

EVENTS

DREAMS

IMAGINATION

DRAFT INSPIRATION

FIGURATIVE LANGUAGE:

1.SIMILE (USE LIKE OR AS)

2.METAPHOR (SAYING ONE IS ANOTHER)

3.PERSONIFICATION(HUMANIZE STUFF)

WRITE NOW & WRITE FREELY

FIND INSPIRATION

WEATHER

_____

_____

_____

SEASON

_____

_____

_____

SIGHTS

_____

_____

_____

SMELL

_____

_____

_____

SOUNDS

_____

_____

_____

TASTE

_____

_____

_____

TOUCH

_____

_____

_____

PEOPLE

_____

_____

_____

BOOKS

_____

_____

_____

EVENTS

_____

_____

_____

DREAMS

_____

_____

IMAGINATION

_____

_____

DRAFT INSPIRATION
FIGURATIVE LANGUAGE:
.SIMILE (USE LIKE OR AS)

.METAPHOR (SAYING ONE IS ANOTHER)

.PERSONIFICATION(HUMANIZE STUFF)

WRITE NOW & WRITE FREELY

FIND INSPIRATION

WEATHER

SEASON

SIGHTS

SMELL

SOUNDS

TASTE

TOUCH

PEOPLE

BOOKS

EVENTS

DREAMS

IMAGINATION

DRAFT INSPIRATION

IGURATIVE LANGUAGE:

.SIMILE (USE LIKE OR AS)

.METAPHOR (SAYING ONE IS ANOTHER)

.PERSONIFICATION(HUMANIZE STUFF)

VRITE NOW & WRITE FREELY

FIND INSPIRATION

WEATHER	SEASON

SIGHTS	SMELL

SOUNDS	TASTE

TOUCH	PEOPLE

BOOKS	EVENTS

DREAMS	IMAGINATION

DRAFT INSPIRATION

FIGURATIVE LANGUAGE:

1.SIMILE (USE LIKE OR AS)

2.METAPHOR (SAYING ONE IS ANOTHER)

3.PERSONIFICATION(HUMANIZE STUFF)

WRITE NOW & WRITE FREELY

FIND INSPIRATION

WEATHER

_____

_____

_____

SEASON

_____

_____

_____

SIGHTS

_____

_____

_____

SMELL

_____

_____

_____

SOUNDS

_____

_____

_____

TASTE

_____

_____

_____

TOUCH

_____

_____

_____

PEOPLE

_____

_____

_____

BOOKS

_____

_____

_____

EVENTS

_____

_____

_____

DREAMS

_____

_____

IMAGINATION

_____

_____

DRAFT INSPIRATION

FIGURATIVE LANGUAGE:

.SIMILE (USE LIKE OR AS)

.METAPHOR (SAYING ONE IS ANOTHER)

.PERSONIFICATION(HUMANIZE STUFF)

WRITE NOW & WRITE FREELY

FIND INSPIRATION

WEATHER

SEASON

SIGHTS

SMELL

SOUNDS

TASTE

TOUCH

PEOPLE

BOOKS

EVENTS

DREAMS

IMAGINATION

DRAFT INSPIRATION

FIGURATIVE LANGUAGE:

.SIMILE (USE LIKE OR AS)

.METAPHOR (SAYING ONE IS ANOTHER)

.PERSONIFICATION(HUMANIZE STUFF)

WRITE NOW & WRITE FREELY

FIND INSPIRATION

WEATHER	SEASON

SIGHTS	SMELL

SOUNDS	TASTE

TOUCH	PEOPLE

BOOKS	EVENTS

DREAMS	IMAGINATION

DRAFT INSPIRATION

FIGURATIVE LANGUAGE:

1.SIMILE (USE LIKE OR AS)

2.METAPHOR (SAYING ONE IS ANOTHER)

3.PERSONIFICATION(HUMANIZE STUFF)

WRITE NOW & WRITE FREELY

FIND INSPIRATION

WEATHER

_____

_____

_____

SEASON

_____

_____

_____

SIGHTS

_____

_____

_____

SMELL

_____

_____

_____

SOUNDS

_____

_____

_____

TASTE

_____

_____

_____

TOUCH

_____

_____

_____

PEOPLE

_____

_____

_____

BOOKS

_____

_____

_____

EVENTS

_____

_____

_____

DREAMS

_____

_____

IMAGINATION

_____

_____

DRAFT INSPIRATION

FIGURATIVE LANGUAGE:

.SIMILE (USE LIKE OR AS)

_____

_____

.METAPHOR (SAYING ONE IS ANOTHER)

_____

_____

.PERSONIFICATION(HUMANIZE STUFF)

_____

_____

WRITE NOW & WRITE FREELY

_____

_____

_____

_____

_____

_____

_____

_____

_____

_____

_____

_____

_____

_____

FIND INSPIRATION

WEATHER

SEASON

SIGHTS

SMELL

SOUNDS

TASTE

TOUCH

PEOPLE

BOOKS

EVENTS

DREAMS

IMAGINATION

DRAFT INSPIRATION

IGURATIVE LANGUAGE:

.SIMILE (USE LIKE OR AS)

.METAPHOR (SAYING ONE IS ANOTHER)

.PERSONIFICATION(HUMANIZE STUFF)

RITE NOW & WRITE FREELY

FIND INSPIRATION

WEATHER

SEASON

SIGHTS

SMELL

SOUNDS

TASTE

TOUCH

PEOPLE

BOOKS

EVENTS

DREAMS

IMAGINATION

DRAFT INSPIRATION

FIGURATIVE LANGUAGE:

1.SIMILE (USE LIKE OR AS)

2.METAPHOR (SAYING ONE IS ANOTHER)

3.PERSONIFICATION(HUMANIZE STUFF)

WRITE NOW & WRITE FREELY

FIND INSPIRATION

WEATHER

SEASON

SIGHTS

SMELL

SOUNDS

TASTE

TOUCH

PEOPLE

BOOKS

EVENTS

DREAMS

IMAGINATION

DRAFT INSPIRATION

IGURATIVE LANGUAGE:

.SIMILE (USE LIKE OR AS)

.METAPHOR (SAYING ONE IS ANOTHER)

.PERSONIFICATION(HUMANIZE STUFF)

VRITE NOW & WRITE FREELY

FIND INSPIRATION

WEATHER

SEASON

SIGHTS

SMELL

SOUNDS

TASTE

TOUCH

PEOPLE

BOOKS

EVENTS

DREAMS

IMAGINATION

DRAFT INSPIRATION

FIGURATIVE LANGUAGE:

.SIMILE (USE LIKE OR AS)

.METAPHOR (SAYING ONE IS ANOTHER)

.PERSONIFICATION(HUMANIZE STUFF)

WRITE NOW & WRITE FREELY

FIND INSPIRATION

WEATHER

SEASON

SIGHTS

SMELL

SOUNDS

TASTE

TOUCH

PEOPLE

BOOKS

EVENTS

DREAMS

IMAGINATION

DRAFT INSPIRATION

FIGURATIVE LANGUAGE:

1.SIMILE (USE LIKE OR AS)

2.METAPHOR (SAYING ONE IS ANOTHER)

3.PERSONIFICATION(HUMANIZE STUFF)

WRITE NOW & WRITE FREELY

FIND INSPIRATION

WEATHER

_____

_____

_____

SEASON

_____

_____

_____

SIGHTS

_____

_____

_____

SMELL

_____

_____

_____

SOUNDS

_____

_____

_____

TASTE

_____

_____

_____

TOUCH

_____

_____

_____

PEOPLE

_____

_____

_____

BOOKS

_____

_____

_____

EVENTS

_____

_____

_____

DREAMS

_____

_____

IMAGINATION

_____

_____

DRAFT INSPIRATION

FIGURATIVE LANGUAGE:

.SIMILE (USE LIKE OR AS)

.METAPHOR (SAYING ONE IS ANOTHER)

.PERSONIFICATION(HUMANIZE STUFF)

WRITE NOW & WRITE FREELY

FIND INSPIRATION

WEATHER

SEASON

SIGHTS

SMELL

SOUNDS

TASTE

TOUCH

PEOPLE

BOOKS

EVENTS

DREAMS

IMAGINATION

DRAFT INSPIRATION

IGURATIVE LANGUAGE:

.SIMILE (USE LIKE OR AS)

.METAPHOR (SAYING ONE IS ANOTHER)

.PERSONIFICATION(HUMANIZE STUFF)

RITE NOW & WRITE FREELY

FIND INSPIRATION

WEATHER	SEASON
SIGHTS	SMELL
SOUNDS	TASTE
TOUCH	PEOPLE
BOOKS	EVENTS
DREAMS	IMAGINATION

DRAFT INSPIRATION

FIGURATIVE LANGUAGE:

1.SIMILE (USE LIKE OR AS)

2.METAPHOR (SAYING ONE IS ANOTHER)

3.PERSONIFICATION(HUMANIZE STUFF)

WRITE NOW & WRITE FREELY

FIND INSPIRATION

WEATHER	SEASON

SIGHTS	SMELL

SOUNDS	TASTE

TOUCH	PEOPLE

BOOKS	EVENTS

DREAMS	IMAGINATION

DRAFT INSPIRATION

IGURATIVE LANGUAGE:

.SIMILE (USE LIKE OR AS)

.METAPHOR (SAYING ONE IS ANOTHER)

.PERSONIFICATION(HUMANIZE STUFF)

RITE NOW & WRITE FREELY

FIND INSPIRATION

WEATHER	SEASON

SIGHTS	SMELL

SOUNDS	TASTE

TOUCH	PEOPLE

BOOKS	EVENTS

DREAMS	IMAGINATION

DRAFT INSPIRATION

FIGURATIVE LANGUAGE:

. SIMILE (USE LIKE OR AS)

_____

_____

. METAPHOR (SAYING ONE IS ANOTHER)

_____

_____

. PERSONIFICATION(HUMANIZE STUFF)

_____

_____

WRITE NOW & WRITE FREELY

_____

_____

_____

_____

_____

_____

_____

_____

_____

_____

_____

_____

_____

_____

FIND INSPIRATION

WEATHER

SEASON

SIGHTS

SMELL

SOUNDS

TASTE

TOUCH

PEOPLE

BOOKS

EVENTS

DREAMS

IMAGINATION

DRAFT INSPIRATION

FIGURATIVE LANGUAGE:

1.SIMILE (USE LIKE OR AS)

2.METAPHOR (SAYING ONE IS ANOTHER)

3.PERSONIFICATION(HUMANIZE STUFF)

WRITE NOW & WRITE FREELY

FIND INSPIRATION

WEATHER	SEASON
SIGHTS	SMELL
SOUNDS	TASTE
TOUCH	PEOPLE
BOOKS	EVENTS
DREAMS	IMAGINATION

DRAFT INSPIRATION

FIGURATIVE LANGUAGE:

.SIMILE (USE LIKE OR AS)

.METAPHOR (SAYING ONE IS ANOTHER)

.PERSONIFICATION(HUMANIZE STUFF)

WRITE NOW & WRITE FREELY

FIND INSPIRATION

WEATHER	SEASON
SIGHTS	SMELL
SOUNDS	TASTE
TOUCH	PEOPLE
BOOKS	EVENTS
DREAMS	IMAGINATION

DRAFT INSPIRATION
FIGURATIVE LANGUAGE:
.SIMILE (USE LIKE OR AS)

.METAPHOR (SAYING ONE IS ANOTHER)

.PERSONIFICATION(HUMANIZE STUFF)

WRITE NOW & WRITE FREELY

FIND INSPIRATION

WEATHER	SEASON

SIGHTS	SMELL

SOUNDS	TASTE

TOUCH	PEOPLE

BOOKS	EVENTS

DREAMS	IMAGINATION

DRAFT INSPIRATION

FIGURATIVE LANGUAGE:

1.SIMILE (USE LIKE OR AS)

2.METAPHOR (SAYING ONE IS ANOTHER)

3.PERSONIFICATION(HUMANIZE STUFF)

WRITE NOW & WRITE FREELY

FIND INSPIRATION

WEATHER

SEASON

SIGHTS

SMELL

SOUNDS

TASTE

TOUCH

PEOPLE

BOOKS

EVENTS

DREAMS

IMAGINATION

DRAFT INSPIRATION

IGURATIVE LANGUAGE:

.SIMILE (USE LIKE OR AS)

.METAPHOR (SAYING ONE IS ANOTHER)

.PERSONIFICATION(HUMANIZE STUFF)

WRITE NOW & WRITE FREELY

FIND INSPIRATION

WEATHER	SEASON
SIGHTS	SMELL
SOUNDS	TASTE
TOUCH	PEOPLE
BOOKS	EVENTS
DREAMS	IMAGINATION

DRAFT INSPIRATION
FIGURATIVE LANGUAGE:

.SIMILE (USE LIKE OR AS)

.METAPHOR (SAYING ONE IS ANOTHER)

.PERSONIFICATION(HUMANIZE STUFF)

WRITE NOW & WRITE FREELY

FIND INSPIRATION

WEATHER	SEASON
SIGHTS	SMELL
SOUNDS	TASTE
TOUCH	PEOPLE
BOOKS	EVENTS
DREAMS	IMAGINATION

DRAFT INSPIRATION

FIGURATIVE LANGUAGE:

1. SIMILE (USE LIKE OR AS)

2. METAPHOR (SAYING ONE IS ANOTHER)

3. PERSONIFICATION (HUMANIZE STUFF)

WRITE NOW & WRITE FREELY

Made in the USA
Las Vegas, NV
20 December 2023

83227070R00046